Self -Hypnosis
Unlocking Your Subconscious Mind
by
Devin Daniels

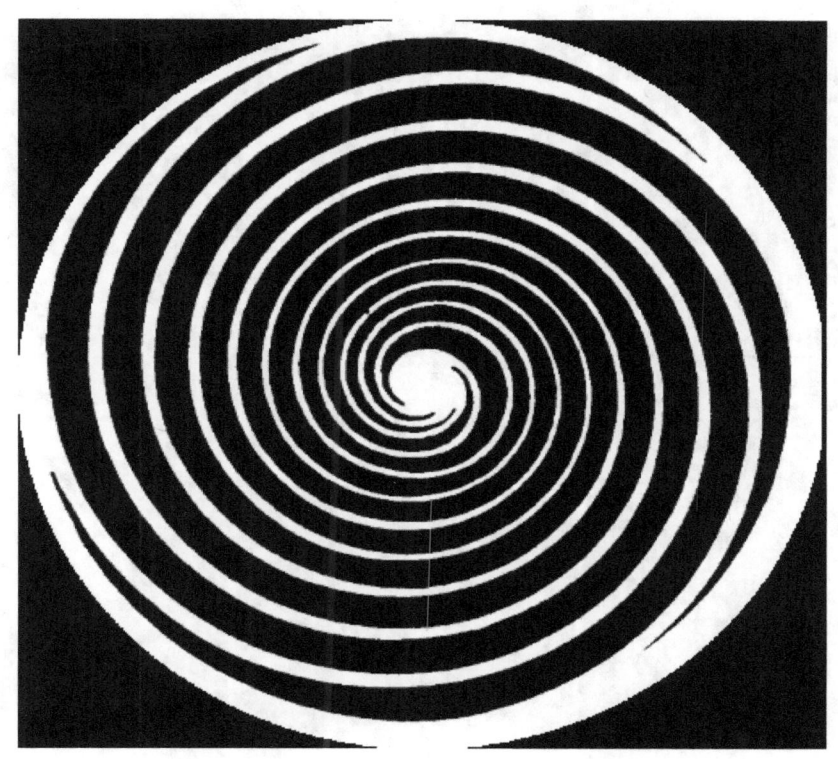

PDP Publications

Copyright 2011 PDP Publications

PDP Publications
http://www.pdppublications.info

First Edition
First Printing 2011
Cover Art by P.Regan

PDP Publications
http://www.pdppublications.info
http://www.pdppublications.com

Table of Contents

Chapter 1: What Self-Hypnosis Is All About

"You are completely relaxed... you feel warm and comfortable ... you feel you really need to close your eyes and sleep... your eyelids are getting heavy... heavier... and heavier... slowly, you close them... now they are closed... you are getting sleepier.... and sleepier.... you are going to SLEEP...... deeper and deeper asleep... SLEEP!"

Thanks to pop culture, hypnotism has achieved a mystical, otherworldly and sometimes evil reputation. While the scenario illustrated above may have a little ring of truth to it (Hypnosis using verbal suggestion is powerful; and people under hypnosis can be made to believe and therefore act as a different identity), there is certainly a lot more than meets the eye about hypnotism.

Self-hypnosis has become one of the hottest ways to help people cope with their addiction. Of course, this is not something that you can use for instance when you are addicted to drugs or when you have a bad case of mental disorder. For the most part, self-hypnosis works for addictions that are not deeply rooted and does not involve any forms of withdrawal.

One of the most common uses of self-hypnosis nowadays is towards self-improvement and personality shift. If you want for instance to suddenly become more patient and manage your anger well, this is the procedure for you. The same goes with people who want to excel academically by enhancing their memory and concentration skills. Self-hypnosis is also found to be effective when it comes to helping relive pain after a medical procedure or when pain is one of the symptoms. There are some that have even used self-hypnosis to quit smoking although it was not completely effective in all of the cases. According to experts, the effectiveness of the procedure will still depend on the individual's own personality and response. There are people who are much easier to hypnotize than others.

Despite its more modern uses, self-hypnosis or hypnosis in general has been part of the world's history since time immemorial. The Egypt for instance found this a good thing and likened it to spiritualism. The Church however does not condone the use of hypnosis and have even been mentioned in the past as one way to open the mind to the devil. New age believers however feel that hypnosis is an untapped science that can help the humankind when utilized better.

Contrary to what most believe, self-hypnosis is safe, perhaps even safer than professionally administered hypnosis because you are basically in control of your own mind. You are not surrendering complete control to the hypnotist. This is good especially if you are not really sure on the abilities of your hypnotist. Doing it yourself can however have a downside. One of them is its slow rate of response. You may need to wait awhile before you can actually notice a change in your behavior. You may have to work real hard for it as opposed to sitting pretty in the company of a professional hypnotist.

This "your own effort" bit is most often what attracts people to self-hypnosis. If you must remember, one of the earlier criticisms against hypnosis is the fact that patients are not essentially changing their behavior but having someone tweak it for them. There is no hard work involved nor there is an intrinsic change to speak of. However, even with the emphasis on doing it on your own, you still need the guidance of a professional hypnotist. In fact before starting the session, you need to get instructions from them. They will also answer all your questions and guide you through your sessions. There is still professional involvement in the sense that they will be monitoring your progress.

On what is more effective, self-hypnosis or professionally-administered, the jury is still out. According to industry experts, a lot depends on the patient who may respond well or not well to a hypnosis session. Still, the mere fact that you can have complete control over yourself even during a hypnosis session already makes self-hypnosis the better choice for most people.

Chapter 2: Is Self-Hypnosis Dangerous?

Many may not be aware that hypnotism occurs to them on a daily basis, but one would still be prompted to ask, is individual hypnosis dangerous?

Many people are yet to recognize whether they are actually being hypnotized or are under a state of hypnosis and surprisingly, it happens often than one would actually think.

Have you ever wondered what happens inside your brain when you are won over by highly convincing sales talk from a sales person or a television or radio advertisement?

Or unwittingly singing along to a commercial jingle playing through a public address system in a grocery or supermarket?

Chances are, and most likely than not, you are being hypnotized.

Although at a much lower degree of hypnosis that affects our everyday life, this is a fact that the state of hypnotism exists.

Most people believe that hypnosis is a world of imagination and a trip down the subconscious realm and spells the difference between imagination and reality.

Of all the many scientific concepts about hypnosis, the most popular of all related concepts is that it is a means of directly accessing the human mind.

One would normally be at a state of mental consciousness, especially during the normal thought process that occur in our brains, like driving, cooking, working in front of a computer or even walking down the aisle of a grocery or supermarket.

Take for example the fact that at the usual and normal state of thought, we mull over problems or think of opportunities as we see and assess them, as well as being conscious of the fact that we are speaking at a particular moment or trying to remember where you may have left a book that you are reading.

But while the conscious mind is at work during the 'conscious' or waking stage, the subconscious mind also works simultaneously in the background by playing a key role in processing the 'subliminal' and 'imaginary' thinking, especially one that affects our spur of the moment decisions or giving in to impulses.

Hypnosis can work both ways, especially with verbal and linguistic programming of suggestive thoughts being introduced to our subconscious thoughts – be it on a positive or negative note.

One effect of negative hypnosis from the normal though process is when a person is swayed from making a decision against his normal or usual better judgment of things or perception.

This is more so evident among people who often get to be adversely affected by thought or opinionated suggestions affecting their self-improvement or self-esteem.

It could also be the result of past experiences of norms handed down from parents that affects one's current state of affairs or efforts for self-improvement.

This can be addressed by gong through hypnosis therapy with a behavioral practitioner or psychiatrist.

The moment a person recognizes the state of hypnosis that affects him; he becomes more familiar with his subconscious thoughts and may be able to 'fix' the pattern of the old hypnotic program that has long affected him.

There are a variety of ways where one can be induced to hypnotism to gradually create a more stable and positive outcome in life, which is one of the best features that can be achieved through hypnotism.

It can come in the form of music, rhythm, repetition, emotion, eye fixation, imagery and authority, among others, which are the most common means of inducing one to a state of hypnotic trance.

After all, hypnosis is a state of deep relaxation and heightened focus, which is but a natural occurrence, but does have its positive effects in the human psyche, especially in dealing with processes in the subconscious mind.

So is individual hypnosis dangerous? Try to weigh the benefits and see for yourself.

Chapter 3: The Benefits of Self Hypnosis

Nowadays, people are now going back to older and natural practices because they know that the modern times have been causing them too much stress. Of all the means of relaxation out there, more and more people are looking forward to experience the benefits of self-hypnosis. Because of its effectivity in terms of calming the mind and developing a person's level of intuition, self hypnosis has now being performed not just a means of clearing the mind and inner reflection but also to heal various illnesses in the mind, emotions, and physical aspects.

Self hypnosis and its benefits

One of the most celebrated benefits of self-hypnosis is that it greatly helps the person's physical state. Among the physical benefits of self-hypnosis involve the heart through a deep rest because it decreases the person's metabolic rate as well as the heart rate, which leads to the reduction of workload for the heart. Also, self-hypnosis can lower the levels of a person's cortisol as well as dissolving the chemicals that are closely associated with everyday stress. Other physical benefits of self-hypnosis include reduced free radicals in the body by eliminating oxygen molecules that are unstable, decreases a person's high blood pressure, develops the ability to have more resistant skin, improve air flow to the lungs to aid easy breathing, and delays biological aging in older people.

When it comes to the psychological factors, self-hypnosis aids in increasing the persons brain wave coherence, decreasing anxiety levels, often irritability, deep-set depression, and mood swings, improves the person's memory as well as his or her learning ability, increases the person's ability for self-actualization, increases the person's feeling of youthfulness and rejuvenation as well as vitality, leads to positive outlook in life and joyfulness, and increases a person's emotional status and stability. Other noted benefits of self-hypnosis for an individual and his or her community include:

- Relaxation to the person's body, mind, and soul,

- Rejuvenation of energy to face the heavy challenges and stress ahead,

- Healing of various illnesses that are closely-associated with the mind and the body,

- Making a more stable person in terms of emotions,

- Developments of relaxed family life and instilling positive outlooks in life to younger people,

- Enhances the person's ability to make his or her mind function properly,

- Letting a person discover his or her inner self, this in turn releases the creativity in the,

- It helps people to free themselves from various vices and addictions such as alcohol and cigarettes as well as in various medications such as tranquilizers and narcotics,

- It also helps a person to gain higher self-confidence, thus, resulting to stronger power of the will,

- It can be an effective and safe way of discovering one's self instead of focusing the attention to other unhealthy practices, and

- It aids in the development of the power of the mind.

The list goes on about the benefits of self-hypnosis in an individual and to his or her community. In so many cases, these are positive benefits but once self-hypnosis has not been used properly, people should be aware of the side effects. To avoid this from happening, people who are planning to get serious in meditation self hypnosis should always consult a professional before performing the practice.

Chapter 4: The Highs and Lows of Self-Hypnosis

Self-hypnosis is a new procedure that is taking the country by storm. Despite being relatively new compared to the usual hypnosis procedures with professionals; self-hypnosis has enjoyed a lot of buzz in recent years. This is perhaps due to the fact that it is completely different from what people usually expect from hypnosis procedures which is a lot of control.

Although the same control can still be seen in self-hypnosis, that control will largely come from the patients themselves. There are no more hypnotists involved that can manipulate you into doing things that you don't want to do and not know that you are doing at all. This time the control and the power to change will be all in your hands. The procedure actually answers two of the things that critic's question about hypnosis itself.

The first one is the idea that a person other than yourself is controlling you and is entering your mind. Mind control is something that people still fear about until now. With self-hypnosis, there will be no hypnotist. Although they will be there to teach you the basics and guide you through the procedure as well as check on your progress, all the hypnosis will be in your hands. You will have control of your own mind, which is how things should be even in real life.

The next thing is the fact that you are not some kind of patsy that will just sit around and let things happen to you through the hypnotist. Now there is an effort coming from the patient itself. Change is no longer something done to you. Now you can do it yourself. A lot of the critics of hypnosis in the first place come from the fact that people are not actively involved in the process. They are only recipients of the cure instead of being the problem solvers themselves.

This is especially true when it is used to curb a bad habit or get over an addiction. When attempting to change, a person should work hard at it otherwise; it will not be a change that comes from something internal. As they say easy come, easy go. Self-hypnosis however changes this fact, as the patients themselves are active problem solvers being the hypnotist themselves.

One downside of self-hypnosis is the fact that an amateur— the patient, who will probably know nothing about hypnosis except that fact that it can somehow solve his problem, does it. Although the hypnotist will be there to guide you, an amateur will still be the one to handle everything and when you really think about it, will any sane person let an amateur get hold of their minds even if those persons are themselves? This is why one of the things that are often asked about self-hypnosis is its safety. According to experts, it is as safe as any hypnosis procedure, maybe even safer because at least this way, you can be sure that you are dealing with someone who is not there to con you.

Another disadvantage of self-hypnosis is the slow progress. Still, responses of people will also depend on whether they are receptive to the task or not. There are people who are more suggestible than other people are and those who are not so suggestible will surely find it hard to find change.

Chapter 5: Awaken Your Senses through Self-Hypnosis

The modern world has brought people a lot of preoccupation. It made living faster yet complicated, it made interactions wider yet shorter, and it made communication easier yet brief. Despite the so many preoccupations brought by media created by people, there are also those who would want to get back to their original self and connect with it in the most basic possible means. One of these is self-hypnosis. Defined as a "process involving a hypnotist and a subject, who agrees to be hypnotized," self-hypnosis is characterized by intense concentration, extreme relaxation, and high suggestibility to both parties.

Experts say that the self-hypnosis is versatile. In fact, its versatility can be quite unparalleled. Today, self hypnosis can take place in various social settings and continue to change social settings dramatically. Unlike before where settings of self-hypnosis are quite limited, today the sessions between the hypnotist and the subject can take place in common places such as clinics, showrooms, classrooms, and even to open spaces and establishments.

Other experts use self hypnosis in order to recover suppressed memories of people who have had bad experiences to help them overcome the problems that they are dealing with right now while other psychologists and hypnotherapists use hypnosis to discover hidden truths from a person's ordinary consciousness. Tapping into the unconscious state or mind where information is believed to dwell does this.

Many perceive that self-hypnosis as a trance-like altered state of a person's consciousness while others believe that it is a way of accessing a person's unconscious mind that is filled to suppressed memories, repressed multiple personalities, various magical insights, and unforgettable memories of the past life. But, in the world of psychology, self-hypnosis is considered as altered state and gateway to knowledge about one's self and the universe he or she is living in.

Today, self-hypnosis is not only used for treating various behavioral problems but also for self-enhancement and improvement. If you are planning to get into hypnosis or self-hypnosis, there are so many things you need to consider. Experts say that self-hypnosis is one of the excellent ways of taking control over one's life. In fact, it can be used as means of disciplining yourself if you want to achieve a specific goal. For some people, self-hypnosis is advisable if you want to achieve something and utmost dedication and discipline is needed. Hypnosis introduction can benefit those who would want to lose or gain weight; those who want to boost their self-confidence; and those who would want to overcome their fears or phobias because it can help them contemplate a lot on the things that they need to do.

If you are planning to get a course on self-hypnosis, you can expect that it can teach you to reach your subconscious mind through bypassing your conscious mind as well as how to communicate with your subconscious mind, methods of creating your own hypnosis scripts and visualizations, how to design and use affirmations, the effects and use of symbols on the subconscious mind, how to understand which methods will be most effective for you personally, deepening your trance state and using visualizations, adapting to scripts to suit various problems, how to change your personal history and plan a more effective future and how to understand your dreams as well.

Chapter 6: Managing Stress through Self-Hypnosis

The stress levels of people now are much higher compared before. This is one of the reasons why more and more of them are finding ways to manage stress so as not to affect their overall health. One of the ways that people—especially those that have super stressful jobs—prefer is self-hypnosis. This is because the practice can help them relieve and manage stress the most natural means possible.

Why use self-hypnosis?

When the word "hypnosis" is mentioned, many people are hesitant to try it because of the common misconception that it can manipulate one to do things beyond his or her wishes. Not many of them realize that this is not always the case. If truth to be told, hypnosis—through self- hypnosis—can be one of the best therapeutic tools that a person can use. This is because people can use this in overcoming their fears. It will also be able to help them in withstanding pain and manage varying levels of stress that they experience in their lives.

Nowadays, the horror of hypnosis is being changed because of the rise in awareness in its seemingly endless possibilities by using it in a therapeutic way. In fact, more and more establishments now are quite open to give hypnosis services to people. This is to prove that hypnosis can be a good thing if it is practiced or conducted by a licensed or a professional hypnotist. It is good to take note the are various types of hypnotists. In the industry of hypnosis, types of hypnotists include showroom hypnotists that usually work in bars and clubs and whose subjects are those people whose idea of good time by joining hundreds of people in places where alcohol is used as a social lubricant and clinical hypnotists, on the other hand, are those who deal with people that have problems and those who consider hypnotherapy as a means of relieving pain and overcoming addiction, fear and confusion.

But, if you still don't have enough trust to other people in hypnotizing you because they might cause you to do something without your consent or proper awareness, it is best to conduct self- hypnosis. This is because you are quite sure that nobody would try to hurt you or make fun of you since you will be conducting it yourself. Aside from ensuring that you are safe, you will also be able to save lots of time and some money since you won't have to travel all the way to a certain clinic and pay for the services of the hypnotist. All you have to do is do some research and you will learn how to use your own voice during the process.

Self-hypnosis as a stress buster

Many people are finding it best to use self-hypnosis as a stress buster because it does not really require so much time, money or effort. In fact, many people would agree that self hypnosis can be one of the easiest means of relieving stress by means of being in a relaxed state where you can directly address the tensions that you feel and somehow trigger your body's response to relaxation. This is helpful to be able to avoid chronic stress that may lead to many health problems. It can also help you achieve a healthier life because it can lead you to develop good habits that can veer you away from activities that have harmful effects not only to your physical body but to your emotional state as well.

Chapter 7: Who Shouldn't use Self-Hypnosis?

You can use self-hypnosis to help you across a range of different areas. Hypnosis isn't for everyone. If you have always felt very nervous about trying it or are convinced it's all a waste of time, it's not going to be very effective. Some people find it hard to become relaxed enough to get to a stage where they are taken deep enough into a quiet state

If that could be you, then before you even start self-hypnosis practice having moments of peace and quiet. Perhaps go on a walk every day without putting on your mp3 player or taking a cell phone or a friend and enjoying the thoughts in your head stop, or try to spend five to ten minutes a day doing nothing but sit quietly. If that is a struggle, relaxing for a self-hypnosis session may prove difficult.

Once that quiet space feels a little easier to get to you can progress to a positive self-hypnosis session. For the new ideas to become well embedded inside your mind, the deeper your level of relaxation the better.

If you have a full chaotic life, consider if you have the time to put into it. Regular sessions are better than one or two every now and again.

If that all sounds a little off putting it doesn't need to be. You'll know when you are ready. If you start and it feels all too stressful take a week or so to break then try again. However, there is one important factor in meeting up with difficulties. Our mind and our bodies like everything to stay the same. The old saying "creatures of habit" is one that perfectly describes all of us. We will do almost anything to stay the same even if the "same" isn't what is best for us. It's one of the reasons so many diets fail. Make big changes all at once and your body starts to protest. It gets scared that it is starting to make changes too fast and won't be able to cope with it.

One of pluses of self-hypnosis is it is something you can do no matter what your current physical state is. Whereas yoga and tai chi can also help you move into a relaxed state, there can be times in your life where that type of movement is not either practical or possible.

The vast majority of people find that the whole journey to new thoughts and actions is pleasantly gentle, encouraging and well worth it. If you want to give it a try, then do, and find out if it suits your needs, your lifestyle and your goals.

Chapter 8: Basic Methods for Self-Hypnosis

As defined, self-hypnosis—also called "autohypnosis"—refers to a form of hypnosis where self-induction is used. Here, the person who practices self-hypnosis uses "autosuggestion" or self-suggestion to be able to adjust or overcome certain conditions or situations. In most cases, self-hypnosis is used as a therapeutic supplement along with hypnotherapy.

Before getting into self-hypnosis the best way to go is to research about it thoroughly. Through research, you can get extensive information about the practice and you will have a better understanding how it would benefit you the most. You can do your research by getting online and surf websites that offer information aligned with the practice. Because of the easy access to information today, you can get almost anything you need to know about it in an instant. In fact, with so many pieces of information about it, you might be overwhelmed. It would be better to be specific on the topics that you really would want to know about so you won't be wasting your time searching for seemingly list of sites.

Aside from the Internet, you can also get information on various books as well as different magazines. Here, you can find interesting articles that can give you a better understanding of the practice especially on the methods that can be used according to the level of skills of the person.

If you are planning to conduct self-hypnosis at home, it is best to ask people who have been practicing it for the basic methods that you can use. If you personally know people who are doing self-hypnosis, it is best to get first hand information from them. Although you can get it also from the practitioners outside, it is still better if you get the facts straight from the people that you know. By doing this, you can get the best tips and advice on how to start with the practice and carry on with it for your personal as well as spiritual growth. Once enough information has been gathered, one can now start with self-hypnosis.

Methods that are being used in self-hypnosis

Experts in this field say that for self-hypnosis to be successful, one should rely on the basic methods and learn them well. A considerable amount of knowledge on the basic methods will somehow help him or her be more familiar with the process and eventually be able to do it easier.

Today, most of the self-hypnosis methods and techniques that are used may include induction procedures, methods for communicating with the subconscious part of the person's mind and suggestion formulation and application. Here are two of the most commonly used methods for self-hypnosis:

1. Self-Hypnosis induction script. This refers to the induction talk for people who will be practicing self-hypnosis. For many people, they can use this as a guide to thinking their way down. In many instances, this is being recorded and can only be listened to during

the practice itself.

2. Autoquestioning. This refers to the set of methods and techniques that are used to get information right from the person's subconscious mind. Many people who practice self hypnosis use its subset, ideomotor questioning the most because the information gathered here are primarily used for correcting suggestions to change as well as acceptance and confirming of the person's subconscious.

Chapter 9: Myths and Truths about Hypnosis

For years, hypnosis has captivated millions of people all over the world from movies, stage shows to urban legends that either makes it a boon or bane to society, but getting to know the myths and truths about group, stage and individual hypnosis will keep us aware that it is indeed a helpful process, rather than a destructive one.

In fact and in truth, there are more misconceptions and myths about hypnosis than any other subject most often talked about by man.

Probably one of the primary reasons for propagating the idea of hypnosis that has greatly affected man's perception is Hollywood, as countless scores of movie plots and stories about hypnosis being a mind control tool to force a subject to do the hypnotist's bidding, be it group, stage or individual hypnosis.

It is best to be aware of knowing how to tell fact from fiction and here are some of the most common misconceptions about hypnosis.

The statement that a hypnotist can make one-do things against their will is totally a figment of one's imagination.

The exact same process and principle for group, stage and individual hypnosis goes for all- they are but one and the same.

This is basically so since a hypnotist does not have mystical powers or absolute authority over the subject, but is merely a guide who leads a subject in going through the stages of the hypnotic state.

Many may not be aware that hypnosis is actually controllable and directed by the subject himself.

The role of the hypnotist as a guide is limited to feeding the subject's mind with key verbal cues or verbal suggestions, which can be ignored or disregarded by the subject at his own will.

Another common statement that subjects under a hypnotic state cannot simply break off from it on his own unless the hypnotist does so is absolutely false.

A subject can break off from the trance –like hypnotic state by either 'walking' up on his own the moment he notices no verbal activity is taking place like the hypnotist staying quiet for a period of time or realizes that the hypnotist leaves the room.

Under this situation, the moment the subject realizes he is alone, will start to open his eyes, as though just having woke up from a deep sleep and feel alert and refreshed.

The subject can also either drift into a deep sleep and wake up after a few minutes or hours, just like having dreamt of the hypnotic process the occurred.

There is also that popular belief that only weak-minded people are the ones that are easily hypnotized.

Chapter 10: Frequently Asked Questions about Self-Hypnosis

Is it true that you can find out more about yourself when you do self-hypnosis?
Yes. Because you will be dealing with the subconscious, you may discover some facts about yourself that you may not know before. This is not some mystical fact or some unconscious secret. For the most part, you will become enlightened on the things that you sometimes hide from yourself. You will even realize hidden motivations and repressed feelings that in some ways can help you become a better person.

Is it safe?
When in the hands of professional hypnotists, it is. The problem is with most reports is the fact that they blame the procedure when it is the individual's fault. News of hypnosis sessions going awry is not the fault of hypnosis as a science but amateur and fake hypnotists. That is why it is important to research the background of hypnotists first before a person even makes an appointment. Remember that this person will have control of your mind for while. If that is not reason enough to really make sure they're legitimate, I don't know what is.

Can self-hypnosis make a person highly suggestible and easily influenced in real life?
Yes to the first question and no to the next. Regular practice of self-hypnosis can

improve a person's response to hypnosis. Sessions will be easier and faster and they will be able to make the most out of their self-hypnosis procedures. You will however be only highly suggestible during your own self-hypnosis sessions. This is because your brain has gotten used to it but if you hypnotize yourself for a completely different thing, it will be back to square one. This is also not something that will spill over your daily grind. People will not become easily influenced just because they practice self-hypnosis. Besides the better that you understand how "suggestions" work, the more you will be knowing how to resist other people's subtle attempts at manipulating you.

What are things that you can use self-hypnosis with?
Some of the most common things that people use self-hypnosis for is changing an existing mindset and personality. A person for instance who easily angers can learn to be patient through self-hypnosis. The same goes with a person who cannot stop talking or gossiping. Students have also used self-hypnosis to improve their grades and enhance learning. Hypnosis is after all can improve one's memory and level of concentration. There are some that have claimed that it also works wonders with relieving pain in the body. Hypnosis can make a person forget about the pain or not feel the pain at all. Although only a few cases of addiction have been associated with self-hypnosis, it has been linked to smoking cessation. Reports however on its effectiveness are still mixed and there is still a need for new data.

Can it improve sports performance? If yes, can it strengthen a person?
Some people have also claimed to use self-hypnosis to improve their performance in sports. This however does not make a person stronger. It cannot affect or change a person's physical make-up. However an improved level of concentration as well as a more fearless attitude may bring on the change in the performance. Fear can sometimes make us hesitate even when we are already doing what comes naturally to us.

Chapter 11: Five Steps to Self-Hypnosis Success

Simply hypnotizing yourself because you want to change something in your life is not going to work, alone. Having a systematic approach before performing self-hypnosis is very helpful. Being clear minded and developing your purpose is just as essential. Being honest with yourself will help you in many ways.

Step 1: Determine what your specific objectives are.

Step 2: Determine what is holding you back from meeting your objectives.

Step 3: Determine why you want to change your ways.

Step 4: Separate Yourself from those things that really aren't you.

Step 5: Be Yourself.

When you have completed the five steps then and only then should you move on to actually performing the act of self-hypnosis.

Chapter 12: Performing Self-Hypnosis

Now that you are aware of what self-hypnosis is all about and how it can affect your life we are ready to perform the task of self-hypnosis. Outlined in this chapter are instructions on how to perform self-hypnosis. I recommend you read through these steps completely to gain an understanding of how to perform each step before actually going through with it.

The method outlines below helps to relax your entire body while ridding yourself of unwanted stress. By having a very relaxed body, you can tremendously improve your life in every aspect – physically, mentally, emotionally, and spiritually.

This self-hypnosis induction suggests that you tape and record the narrative and play it during your session, in accordance to the whole therapy process. In this session, the subject is instructed to keep their eyes open initially, watching the flickering flame of a candle.

Self-Hypnosis Induction

Light up a candle place it in front of you, where you can see the flame at a Convenient angle.

Find a comfortable sitting position. Surround yourself with pillows and blankets if you must.

The mellow light of the flame: watch it dance and sway slowly, languidly, peacefully, as you are feeling now. (Pause)

Breath in, breath out. Breathe through your nose and faintly blow out some air from your slightly open mouth. (Pause)

Breath in, breath out. (Pause)

Repeat. Breath in, breathe out. Breathe in, and out. (Pause)

Breathe and take the wonderful air into your healthy lungs. Feel it being filled with sweet, clean air. (Pause)

Exhale and blow out all your tension away from your body. (Pause)

Breathe. Relax. As relaxed and as languid as the flickering flame before you. (Pause)

The flame is mellow. Its light is yellow, like the stars, like when you sleep. The flame warms your eyes. You feel them closing slowly. (Pause)

Your eyes are tired, so weighed down. You feel all the nerves inside your eyes throbbing. You want to close your eyes tightly. (Pause)

Your eyes still feel warm. You feel the heat of the flame surround them. In fact, even with eyes closed, you can clearly see the flame dancing before you. (Pause)

You breathe in and out. The more you breathe, the more you feel relaxed, very deeply now. (Pause)

The warmth spreads from your eyes to your face. You feel warm all over. (Pause)

You feel your forehead glowing. A light, luminous and bright, shines from your forehead. (Pause)

The warm, soft light spreads to your face. You face relaxes. You relax deeper and deeper now. (Pause)

As you breathe in and out, you feel more relaxed than ever. (Pause)

You breathe and you feel your chest filled with air. Warm air. The light from your face spreads to your neck down to the chest. (Pause)

Breathe deeply now. The warm, soft light makes your body relaxed, as relaxed as your face. (Pause)

The warm, soft, relaxing light spreads to your arms, to your hands, to the tips of your fingertips. They feel so relaxed now. (Pause)

The warm, soft, relaxing light spreads down to your stomach, to your waist, to your hips. They feel so relaxed now. (Pause)

The warm, soft, relaxing light spreads further down to your back. Your back feels so relaxed now. (Pause)

You breathe slowly and deeply, in and out. More than ever, you feel so relaxed now. (Pause)

The warm, soft, relaxing light spreads further down to your thighs, to your legs. They feel so relaxed now. All the weight put upon them slowly feels light. (Pause)

You feel so relaxed. Every muscle, every tissue in your body feels so fine. You feel so peaceful. (Pause)

You breathe in and out. You go deeper and deeper into relaxation. (Pause)

The warm, soft, relaxing light spreads further down to your feet, to the tips of your toes. They feel so relaxed now. All the weight put upon them slowly feels light. (Pause)

Now visualize yourself standing in the softest, greenest grass you have ever put your feet into. Your feet feel warm and soft. (Pause)

You are now in an open field. The sun is shining warmly, so friendly on you. (Pause)

A cool wind breezes through your hair, your face, and your body. It breezes through the field of grass, combing each and every soft, green sliver. (Pause)

You walk through the field of soft, warm grass. You see a mountain not far way. You slowly walk towards the mountain. (Pause)

As you walk towards the warm, blue mountain, you go deeper and deeper into relaxation. You body feels so relaxed and at ease. (Pause)

Your mind is sharp and alert, taking each and every detail perfectly. (Pause) Perfectly, like the little stream you pass by on the way. The gurgling sound of the stream relaxes you more than ever. You walk across the little stream, your feet getting wet by the warm, clear water. The water relaxes you more that ever. (Pause)

You walk, further and further, into the mountain. (Pause)

A warm, gentle breeze passes you by, combing your hair, passing through your clothes and your body, and slowly, slowly lifting you, as if you are a feather in the air. (Pause)

The wind lifts you and you feel so fine floating in the sweet, soft air. You feel weightless and you go deeper and deeper into relaxation. (Pause)

You go higher and higher until you reach the top of the mountain. (Pause)

There are small wild flowers on the top of the mountain. You breathe in their wonderful, fresh smell. You breathe in the wonderful, fresh smell of the mountain breeze. (Pause)

The wind slowly, slowly gets you down the mountain. As you get lower and lower you become more aware. With every count you start to slowly emerge from your deep relaxation. (Pause)

Every time you listen to this self-hypnosis induction you will go deeper, more serenely, and attain more benefits from the experience. (Pause)

1, 2, 3…

The smell of the soft, fresh rain is still in you. It's in your hair, your hands, your body. You smell of rain. You smell of new hope, of creation and of refreshed life.

4. 5, 6,

Lower, into the field of grass. Lower, until your feet touch the warm soft grass once more.

By the count of ten, you will completely be awake, more alive and refreshed than ever before.

7,8,9,

Remember the smell of rain and how it brings out new life, new hope.

10

You awake fresh and ready. Yawn and stretch your body.

Chapter 13: Conclusion

"I think therefore I am," philosopher Rene Descartes once said a long time ago. Following his discourse that anything is real once you set your mind to it, then indeed, hypnosis may just be the logical step to achieving the best version of yourself.

The power of the mind and the subconscious: boundless and as generous as your dreams. Tapping that power through hypnosis is looking inside you and knowing your capabilities. It means understanding yourself, the people around you, and the world you live in. It is realizing that life and living is never constant. It is appreciating that we always aspire for change – and that change happens from your willingness, your initiative, your hard work and perseverance.

Remember: Change is a verb. It fulfills its meaning once you act on it.

As repeatedly stated all throughout this report, we claim no guarantee that this e-book will change your life.

You may have realized that by this time, IT ALL DEPENDS ON YOU.

You have the power within you. And no one can take it away from you. Self-hypnosis helps you unleash and harness that power.

Given that you have regularly applied and practiced the prescriptions here – the process in itself is as important than the product.

You learned how to unease your burden. You took time for yourself. You made an effort to look within yourself to examine your thoughts and live with its rewards and consequences. Congratulations and good luck with your hypnosis sessions.

Disclaimer

First Edition

First Printing 2011

Cover Art by P.Regan

PDP Publications

http://www.pdppublications.info

http://www.pdppublications.com

PDP Publications

Copyright 2011 PDP Publications

PDP Publications
http://www.pdppublications.info

33